500 **words**
Level 2

白蛇的传说

Legend of the White Snake

许晓华 改编　张乐 翻译

MP3
Download Online

Sinolingua
华语教学出版社

First Edition   2016
Fifth Printing   2022

ISBN 978-7-5138-1000-5
Copyright 2016 by Sinolingua Co., Ltd
Published by Sinolingua Co., Ltd
24 Baiwanzhuang Street, Beijing 100037, China

Tel: (86) 10-68320585   68997826
Fax: (86) 10-68997826   68326333
http://www.sinolingua.com.cn
E-mail: hyjx@sinolingua.com.cn
Facebook: www.facebook.com/sinolingua
Printed by Beijing Hucais Culture Communication Co., Ltd

Printed in the People's Republic of China

编者的话

对于广大汉语学习者来说，要想快速提高汉语水平，扩大阅读量是很有必要的。"彩虹桥"汉语分级读物为汉语学习者提供了一系列有趣、有用的汉语阅读材料。本系列读物按照词汇量进行分级，并通过精彩的故事叙述，给读者带来了丰富有趣的阅读享受。本套读物主要有以下特点：

一、分级精准，循序渐进。我们参考了新汉语水平考试（HSK）词汇表（2012 年修订版）、《汉语国际教育用音节汉字词汇等级划分（国家标准）》和《常用汉语 1500 高频词语表》等词汇分级标准，结合《欧洲语言教学与评估框架性共同标准》（CEFR），设计了一套适合汉语学习者的"彩虹桥"词汇分级标准。本系列读物分为 7 个级别（入门级*、1 级、2 级、3 级、4 级、5 级、6 级），供不同水平的汉语学习者选择，每个级别故事的生词数量不超过本级别对应词汇量的 20%。随着级别的升高，故事的篇幅逐渐加长。本系列读物与 HSK、CEFR 的对应级别，各级词汇量以及每本书的字数详见下表。

*　入门级（Starter）在封底用 S 标识。

级别	入门级	1级	2级	3级	4级	5级	6级
对应级别	HSK1 CEFR A1	HSK1-2 CEFR A1-A2	HSK2-3 CEFR A2-B1	HSK3 CEFR A2-B1	HSK3-4 CEFR B1	HSK4 CEFR B1-B2	HSK5 CEFR B2-C1
词汇量	150	300	500	750	1 000	1 500	2 500
字数	1 000	2 500	5 000	7 500	10 000	15 000	25 000

二、故事精彩，题材多样。本套读物选材的标准就是"精彩"，所选的故事要么曲折离奇，要么感人至深，对读者构成奇妙的吸引力。选题广泛取材于中国的神话传说、民间故事、文学名著、名人传记和历史故事等，让汉语学习者在阅读中潜移默化地了解中国的文化和历史。

三、结构合理，实用性强。"彩虹桥"系列读物的每一本书中，除了中文故事正文之外，都配有主要人物的中英文介绍、生词英文注释及例句、故事正文的英文翻译、练习题以及生词表，方便读者阅读和理解故事内容，提升汉语阅读能力。练习题主要采用客观题，题型多样，难度适中，并附有参考答案，既可供汉语教师在课堂上教学使用，又可供汉语学习者进行自我水平检测。

如果您对本系列读物有什么想法，比如推荐精彩故事、提出改进意见等，请发邮件到 liuxiaolin@sinolingua.com.cn，与我们交流探讨。也可以关注我们的微信公众号 CHQRainbowBridge，随时与我们交流互动。同时，微信公众号会不定期发布有关"彩虹桥"的出版信息，以及汉语阅读、中国文化小知识等。

韩　颖　刘小琳

Preface

For students who study Chinese as a foreign language, it's crucial for them to enlarge the scope of their reading to improve their comprehension skills. The "Rainbow Bridge" Graded Chinese Reader series is designed to provide a collection of interesting and useful Chinese reading materials. This series grades each volume by its vocabulary level and brings the learners into every scene through vivid storytelling. The series has the following features:

I. A gradual approach by grading the volumes based on vocabulary levels. We have consulted the New HSK Vocabulary (2012 Revised Edition), the *Graded Chinese Syllables, Characters and Words for the Application of Teaching Chinese to the Speakers of Other Languages (National Standard)* and the 1500 Commonly Used High Frequency Chinese Vocabulary, along with the Common European Framework of Reference for Languages (CEFR) to design the "Rainbow Bridge" vocabulary grading standard. The series is divided into seven levels (Starter*, Level 1, Level 2, Level 3, Level 4, Level 5 and Level 6) for students at different stages in their Chinese education to choose from. For each level, new words are no more than 20% of the vocabulary amount as specified in the corresponding HSK and CEFR levels.

---

*   Represented by "S" on the back cover.

As the levels progress, the passage length will in turn increase. The following table indicates the corresponding "Rainbow Bridge" level, HSK and CEFR levels, the vocabulary amount, and number of characters.

Level	Starter	1	2	3	4	5	6
HSK/ CEFR Level	HSK1 CEFR A1	HSK1-2 CEFR A1-A2	HSK2-3 CEFR A2-B1	HSK3 CEFR A2-B1	HSK3-4 CEFR B1	HSK4 CEFR B1-B2	HSK5 CEFR B2-C1
Vocabulary	150	300	500	750	1000	1500	2500
Characters	1000	2500	5000	7500	10,000	15,000	25,000

II. Intriguing stories on various themes. The series features engaging stories known for their twists and turns as well as deeply touching plots. The readers will find it a joyful experience to read the stories. The topics are selected from Chinese mythology, legends, folklore, literary classics, biographies of renowned people and historical tales. Such widely ranged topics would exert an invisible, yet formative, influence on readers' understanding of Chinese culture and history.

III. Reasonably structured and easy to use. For each volume of the "Rainbow Bridge" series, apart from a Chinese story, we also provide an introduction to the main characters in Chinese and English, new words with English explanations and sample sentences, and an English translation of the story, followed by comprehension exercises and a vocabulary list to help users read and understand the story and improve their Chinese reading skills. The exercises are mainly presented as objective questions that take on various forms with moderate difficulty. Moreover, keys to the exercises are also provided. The series can be used by teachers in class or by students for self-study.

If you have any questions, comments or suggestions about the series, please email us at liuxiaolin@sinolingua.com.cn. You can also exchange ideas with us via our WeChat account: CHQRainbowBridge. This account will provide updates on the series along with Chinese reading materials and cultural tips.

Han Ying and Liu Xiaolin

主要人物和地点
Main Characters and Places

许　仙 (Xǔ Xiān)：一个年轻小伙子。他见到白素贞以后，爱上了她，后来他和她结婚了。

Xu Xian: A young man who fell in love with Bai Suzhen after their encounter. Later, the two of them got married.

白素贞 (Bái Sùzhēn)：也叫白娘子，一个漂亮姑娘，以前是一条白蛇。她见到许仙以后，爱上了他，后来她和他结婚了。

Bai Suzhen (Madam White): A beautiful woman who used to be a white snake. She fell in love with Xu Xian and married him.

小　青 (Xiǎoqīng)：白素贞的妹妹，以前是一条青蛇。

Xiao Qing: The younger sister of Bai Suzhen. She used to be a green snake.

法　海 (Fǎhǎi)：一个坏和尚。他很不喜欢白素贞和小青。

Fahai:　An evil Buddhist monk who disliked Bai Suzhen and Xiao Qing.

杭　州 (Hángzhōu)：中国南方的一个城市。

Hangzhou: A city in the southern part of China.

西　湖 (Xī Hú)：杭州城里的一个大湖，风景很美。

West Lake: A big lake in Hangzhou, it is well-known for its picturesque scenery.

白蛇①的传说②

① 蛇 (shé) *n.* snake
e.g., 今天，我看见一条蛇。

② 传说 (chuánshuō) *n.* legend
e.g., 这是一个有名的传说。

③ 南方 (nánfāng) *n.* south
e.g., 在中国，南方比北方热。

④ 风景 (fēngjǐng) *n.* scenery
e.g., 听说那个公园的风景很美，我想去看看。

⑤ 美丽 (měilì) *n.* beautiful, pretty
e.g., 这是一个美丽的传说。

⑥ 湖 (hú) *n.* lake
e.g., 这个湖里有很多鱼。

⑦ 古代 (gǔdài) *n.* ancient times
e.g., 古代的衣服跟现在的不一样。

中国南方③有一个城市，叫杭州。那儿的风景④非常美丽⑤，每年都有很多人去那里旅游。杭州最美的地方是一个美丽的湖⑥，叫西湖。许仙与白娘子的故事就发生在西湖。这是中国古代⑦一个很有名的爱情故事。许仙是一个年轻

的小伙子①，白娘子名叫白素贞，是一位美丽的姑娘。不过这位姑娘以前是一条白蛇——蛇可以变成人吗？在中国的传说里，是可以的。

第一次见面

那一天，天气非常好，西湖边来了很多人，大家都是来看美丽的风景的。四月的西湖是一年中最美的，花开了，树绿②了，阳

① 小伙子 (xiǎohuǒzi) *n.* young man
e.g., 这个小伙子的女朋友很漂亮。

② 绿 (lǜ) *adj.* green
e.g., 公园的树是绿的。

① 暖 (nuǎn) *adj.*
warm
e.g., 今天天气很好，
阳光暖暖的。

② 散步 (sànbù) *v.*
take a walk
e.g., 晚饭以后，我
们出去散散步吧。

③ 划船 (huáchuán) *v.*
boat
e.g., 星期六，我想
去公园划船。

光暖①暖的，人们也都开开心心的。有的在湖边散步②，有的在湖上划船③，有的在看花，有的在看树，有的在看水里的鱼。

在这些人中，有两个美丽的姑娘，她们也跟大家一样，一边走，一边看，一边说，一边笑。这两个姑娘，一个穿着白色的衣服，一个穿着绿色的衣服，都长得很漂亮，很多从她们身边走过的人，都会多看她们几眼。没有人知道，这两个姑娘其实^①是蛇变的。穿白衣服的姑娘，以前是一条白蛇，穿绿衣服的姑娘，以前是一条青蛇。白蛇变成的姑娘，叫白素

① 其实 (qíshí) *adv.*
actually; in fact
e.g., 他说喜欢看书，其实不是真的。

① 练功 (liàngōng)
v. practice magical arts; practice one's skill
e.g., 他每天都认真地练功，所以身体很好。

② 法力 (fǎlì) *n.*
magic power
e.g., 这个人的法力很大，大家都怕他。

③ 伞 (sǎn) *n.*
umbrella
e.g., 下雨了，我有两把伞，给你一把吧。

④ 湿 (shī) *adj.* wet
e.g., 衣服湿了，我要去换衣服。

⑤ 到处 (dàochù) *n.* every place; all places
e.g., 星期天，公园里到处都是人。

⑥ 躲 (duǒ) *v.* hide, duck
e.g., 我不喜欢他，看见他就躲。

贞；青蛇变成的姑娘，叫小青。白素贞是姐姐，小青是妹妹。蛇怎么会变成人呢？原来她们不是一般的蛇，已经有一千多岁了，她们用了一千年在山上练功①，终于有了很大的法力②，变成了美丽的姑娘。她们早就听说西湖很美，今天天气很好，就一起出来玩儿了。

她们正高兴地说笑，突然下起雨来了。早上天气好好的，她们没想到中午会下雨，所以没带伞③。雨下得很大，不一会儿，她们的衣服就湿④了，她们只好到处⑤跑，想找个地方躲⑥雨。她们跑着跑着，突然觉得头上的雨停了，这是怎么回事呢？两人抬头①一看，头上多了一把伞。给她们打伞的，是一个又年轻又帅②的小伙子。小伙子只有一把伞，为了给她们打伞，自己的衣服都湿了。小伙子安静③地站着，什么话也不说。白素贞看着他，他也看着白素贞，谁也不说话，可是两个人都觉得对方④很面熟⑤，像在哪儿见过。

小青站在旁边，看着他们两个人笑了。她说："你们两个以前认识？"两个人的脸一下子都红了。小青忙说："我开玩笑呢！我知道姐姐不认识你。请问，你叫什么名字？是杭州人吗？"小伙子忙说："我叫

① 抬头 (tái tóu) v. raise one's head
e.g., 他抬头看天，天很蓝。

② 帅 (shuài) adj. handsome
e.g., 他长得很帅，喜欢他的人很多。

③ 安静 (ān jìng) adj. quiet, calm
e.g., 房间里没有一个人，很安静。

④ 对方 (duìfāng) n. other side; other party
e.g., 他们两个人每天见面，可是都不知道对方的名字。

⑤ 面熟 (miànshú) adj. (of a person's appearance) familiar
e.g., 我觉得你很面熟，我们见过面吗？

① 聊 (liáo) *v.* chat
e.g., 昨天，我和朋友聊得很开心。

许仙，就住在西湖边。请问，两位姑娘是……"小青说："我叫小青，这是我姐姐白素贞。我们住在杭州外边。今天出来玩，没想到会下雨。谢谢你的伞啦！"她们和许仙又聊① 了一会儿。雨停了，小青拉着姐姐走了。许仙一直站在那里，看着她们一点点走远，走远。

结　婚

回到家，<u>小青</u>对<u>白素贞</u>说："姐姐，今天你一直在看那个<u>许仙</u>，你是不是喜欢上他了？"<u>白素贞</u>没说话，可是脸红了。过了一会儿，她说："唉①！我喜欢他有什么用呢？我们是蛇，他是人，我们跟他不一样。蛇和人怎么能在一起呢？"<u>小青</u>说："我已经看出来了，你喜欢他，他也喜欢

① 唉 (āi) *interj.* (used to express sadness or regret) alas
e.g., 唉，我又没有钱了。

① 互相 (hùxiāng)
adv. mutually; each other
e.g., 我想学汉语，他想学英语，我们可以互相学习。

你。你们互相①喜欢，为什么不能在一起呢？我们以前是蛇，可是现在变成人了啊！"白素贞听了小青的话，觉得她说得也对。

第二天，白素贞和小青又去西湖边散步，她们希望能再次见到许仙。她们刚走了一会儿，就看见许仙向她们走过来。原来，许仙和她们想的一样，他也想再次见到那个穿白衣服的姑娘。三个人一见面，都笑了。

他们像老朋友一样，一边散步，一边聊天。这一天，他们聊了很长时间。白素贞和小青知道了很多许仙的事情。他的父母已经死了，哥哥姐姐也都结婚了，现在家里只有他一个人住。他是个读书人，每天在家看书、写字。因为住在西湖边，他看书看累了，就来湖边散一会儿步。后来，他们差不多每天都在西湖边见面，每次白素贞和许仙都会聊很长时间，每次都聊得很开心。一天天过去了，白素贞和许仙的感情①越来越好，他们越来越喜欢对方了。

三个月后，他们决定结婚了。结婚这天，许仙请

① 感情 (gǎnqíng)
n. emotion, feeling, sentiment
e.g., 我爱爸爸、妈妈，我们三个人感情很好。

① 温柔 (wēnróu)
adj. gentle and soft; sweet
e.g., 她很温柔，大家都很喜欢她。

② 运气 (yùnqi) *n.*
luck, fortune
e.g., 最近我的运气不好，不好的事都来找我了。

③ 实在 (shízài) *adv.*
indeed
e.g., 每次我有问题，他都帮我。他实在太好了！

④ 家务 (jiāwù) *n.*
chore, housework
e.g., 我不喜欢做家务。

了很多朋友。朋友们看到白素贞又温柔①又美丽，都说，许仙的运气②实在③太好了。结婚以后，小青也住在许仙的家里。白天，许仙在家里看书、写字，白素贞和小青就一边聊天，一边做家务④。许仙看书看累了，三个人就一起到西湖边一边散步，一边聊天。他们生活得非常幸福，非常快乐。

11

开药店 ①

这一天，<u>白素贞</u>正在家做家务，突然听到邻居家孩子的哭声。孩子的哭声很大，好像是生病了。<u>白素贞</u>过去一看，孩子发烧②了，嗓子③很疼④，咳嗽⑤得很厉害⑥。孩子的妈妈对她说，孩子病了，可是她没钱带孩子去看病，而且大

① 药店 (yàodiàn) *n.*
pharmacy
e.g., 我要去药店买药。

② 发烧 (fāshāo) *v.*
have a fever
e.g., 他发烧了，40℃。

③ 嗓子 (sǎngzi) *n.*
throat
e.g., 他的嗓子很红。

④ 疼 (téng) *v.* hurt,
ache
e.g., 他的头很疼。

⑤ 咳嗽 (késou) *v.*
cough
e.g., 他病了，今天一直在咳嗽。

⑥ 厉害 (lìhai) *adj.*
serious, intense
e.g., 他病得很厉害，要去医院。

① 摸 (mō) *v.* feel, stroke, touch
e.g., 妈妈用手摸了摸我的头，笑了。

② 挣钱 (zhèng qián) make money; gain profit
e.g., 今年我工作了，开始挣钱了。

③ 医术 (yīshù) *n.* medical skill
e.g., 他是个好大夫，医术很好。

夫家离她家太远。白素贞看了看孩子的脸，又摸①了摸孩子的手。她想了想，就跑着去了一家药店。她在药店买了药，回来让孩子吃。第二天，孩子的病就好了。孩子的妈妈对很多人说，白素贞是个好大夫，看好了她孩子的病。很快，这件事大家都知道了。后来，很多人生病了，就来找白素贞，她每次都帮大家看病、开药。

后来，白素贞和许仙说，她想开一家药店。许仙家没有很多钱，开药店可以挣钱②，还可以帮助那些没有钱看病的人。白素贞练功练了一千多年，法力很大，所以她的医术③

也很好。有的人病了，看了很多大夫，吃了很多药，病都没有好。可是，来到<u>白素贞</u>的药店，吃了她开的药，一两天后，这些人的病就都好了。后来，大家只要有病，就都来找她看病、开药。来找她看病的人越来越多，药店的生意① 也一天比一天好。那些

① 生意 (shēngyi) *n.* business
e.g., 这家商店的生意很好，每天都有很多人去买东西。

14

① 金山寺 (Jīnshān
Sì) *n.* Gold Mountain
Temple

② 和尚 (héshang) *n.*
Buddhist monk
e.g., 他是个和尚。

③ 上香 (shàngxiāng)
v. burn incense and
worship
e.g., 她希望能有个
孩子，所以去金山寺
上香了。

④ 香火钱
(xiānghuǒqián) *n.*
donations to a
temple
e.g., 上香的人常常
给一些香火钱。

没有钱的人来看病，白素贞从来不要钱。大家都很喜欢她，因为她常常穿白色的衣服，所以大家都叫她"白娘子"。

药店的生意很好，许仙和白素贞的生活也很幸福。可是有一个人不高兴了。他是谁呢？他就是金山寺①的一个和尚②，叫法海。因为以前，人们家里有人病了，就会到金山寺来上香③，还会给很多香火钱④。可是最近几个月，来金山寺上香的人比以前少多了，香火钱也越来越少了。法海不知道这是为什么。他出去问了几个认识的人，这才知道原因。别人告诉他，现在人们病了，

都去找白娘子。白娘子很
厉害，什么病都能治① 好，
卖的药也不贵。要是看病
时没有钱，她就不要钱了。
有这样的好大夫，当然就
不用去金山寺上香了。原
来，庙② 里的香火钱越来越
少，就是因为这个白娘子
啊！法海很生气。

① 治 (zhì) v. cure,
heal
e.g., 这个大夫治好
了很多人的病。
② 庙 (miào) n. temple
e.g., 他是这庙里的
一个和尚。

① 现形 (xiànxíng)
v. reveal one's true features
e.g., 这个女人喝了一点酒，就现形了，变成了一条蛇。

白蛇现形 ①

　　第二天，法海决定去白娘子的药店看一看，看看这个女人长什么样，医术怎么会这么好！他来到白素贞的药店时，她正在给人看病，药店门口还有很多人在等着。法海也是一个有法术的人。他看了一

许家药店

会儿，就发现了问题：这个白娘子不是一般的人，她是一条白蛇变的！

他在药店外面站了一会儿，想出了一个主意①。他去了许仙的家，对许仙说："你的妻子不是人，是白蛇变的。你快点和她分开吧，要不，她以后会吃了你！"许仙不相信，说："我的妻子是最好的女人！她人好，心也好。你为什

① 主意 (zhǔyi) *n.*
idea
e.g., 我有个好主意。

① 雄黄酒 (xióng-huángjiǔ) *n.* realgar liquor, liquor mixed with foul-smelling realgar to drive away snakes

② 试 (shì) *v.* try e.g., 这件衣服很好看，你试试。

③ 不安 (bù'ān) *adj.* uneasy, disturbed e.g., 很晚了，女儿还没回家，妈妈很不安。

么说她是白蛇？"法海说："我就知道你不相信。这样吧，今天回家以后，你买一些雄黄酒①给她喝，她喝了酒，就会变成白蛇。要不，你试②试？"

许仙不想相信法海的话，可是心里很不安③。法海走了以后，许仙想了两天。这两天，他不想吃饭，不想睡觉，妻子跟他聊天，他也不想说话。两天以后，他决定试一试。他想，妻子一定不是白蛇，喝点儿酒应该没问题。这样试过以后，他就不会觉得不安了。第三天，他去买了雄黄酒，还买了很多菜。他做好饭等着妻子回来。

白素贞回家了，许仙

高兴地对她说："最近你太累了。今天我做了几个你爱吃的菜。我们喝点儿酒吧！"最近两天，<u>白素贞</u>看到<u>许仙</u>不开心，不知道为什么，正有点儿担心①呢。现在看<u>许仙</u>高兴，她也很高兴，所以就同意喝酒了。她当然不知道<u>许仙</u>的想法②。可是她一看是雄

① 担心 (dānxīn) *v.*
be worried
e.g., 我一个人来中国，妈妈有点儿担心。

② 想法 (xiǎngfǎ) *n.*
idea
e.g., 我和你的想法不一样。

20

① 办法 (bànfǎ) *n.*
solution
e.g., 你帮我想一个
办法吧。

② 桌子 (zhuōzi) *n.*
table, desk
e.g., 我想买一张
桌子。

③ 床 (chuáng) *n.*
bed
e.g., 他的房间里有
一张床。

④ 吓 (xià) *v.* frighten;
be scared
e.g., 爸爸生气了,
我吓哭了。

黄酒,就把酒杯放下了,说她不想喝这种酒。

许仙说:"这种酒很好喝,你就喝一点儿吧。"许仙说了一次又一次,白素贞没办法①,只好喝了一小口。她想,只喝一小口,可能没问题吧。没想到,只一会儿,她就觉得头疼得厉害。她知道,出了大问题。她想让许仙出去,可是已经说不出话了。

许仙站在桌子②旁边,看到妻子的脸越来越红,像生病了一样。他想让她到床③上休息。可是,他看到妻子的身体在变,一点点地变,一会儿就变成了一条大白蛇。许仙吓④坏了,大叫了一声,倒在了

地上。

白娘子救^①丈夫

夜里^②，白蛇变回了白娘子。她看到许仙倒在地上，过去一看，他已经死了。白素贞知道，是自己吓死了丈夫，她一下子急^③哭了。这时候，小青也回来了。她对姐姐说，她知

① 救 (jiù) v. save, rescue
e.g., 请你救救我，我不会游泳。

② 夜里 (yèli) n. night
e.g., 这个地方，白天很热，夜里很冷。

③ 急 (jí) v. be anxious
e.g., 你别急，我知道你的书在哪儿。

① 灵芝草
(língzhīcǎo) *n.* ganoderma mushroom

② 野兽 (yěshòu) *n.* beast; wild animal e.g., 山上有野兽，我不想去。

道有一种灵芝草①，可以救活许仙。这种灵芝草长在昆仑山上。可是那座山很高，山上有很多可怕的野兽②，离西湖也很远。白素贞说，她一定要去找灵芝草，山高，她不怕；野兽，她也不怕；路远，也没关系。她一定要救活许仙！

第二天，白素贞出发

了。她一路上不吃饭，不睡觉，几天后终于到了<u>昆仑山</u>①。她打跑了野兽，<u>爬</u>②到山上最高的地方，找到了<u>灵芝草</u>。她的衣服<u>破</u>③了，手<u>脚</u>④<u>流血</u>⑤了，人也<u>瘦</u>⑥了很多。她非常累，真想休息一下。可是她心里想着<u>许仙</u>，一会儿也没有

① 昆仑山 (Kūnlún Shān) *n.* Kunlun Mountains

② 爬 (pá) *v.* climb
e.g., 他喜欢爬山。

③ 破 (pò) *v.* break, damage
e.g., 这件衣服穿了很多年了，有两个地方破了。

④ 脚 (jiǎo) *n.* foot
e.g., 我脚疼，不能走路了。

⑤ 流血 (liú xiě) *v.* bleed
e.g., 昨天，我的手流了很多血。

⑥ 瘦 (shòu) *adj.* thin
e.g., 你太瘦了，多吃一点儿吧。

休息，很快就回家了。

　　许仙吃了灵芝草以后，一下子就活了。小青哭了，她告诉许仙，是白素贞救了他。为了救他，白素贞走了很远的路，吃了很多苦，终于找到了灵芝草。白素贞也哭了。她说："对不起，以前我没有告诉

你，我是一条白蛇，你是被我吓死的。"许仙哭了。他说："我现在知道你多么爱我了。你是白蛇，没关系①！我要和你一直在一起，不会离开你。"

后来，他们的生活又跟以前一样了。白天，白素贞和小青去药店，许仙有时候去药店帮忙，有时候在家看书。他们还是常常去西湖，在湖边一边散步，一边聊天。几个月之后，白素贞怀孕②了。要当爸爸了，许仙很高兴，也更爱自己的妻子了。

水漫③金山寺

有一天，白素贞去了药店，许仙一个人去看朋友。在路上，他看见了法海。

① 没关系 (méi guānxi) it doesn't matter ... e.g., 你没有钱，没关系，我给你钱。

② 怀孕 (huáiyùn) v. be pregnant e.g., 她怀孕了，要做妈妈了。

③ 漫 (màn) v. overflow, flood; run over e.g., 雨很大，一会儿就漫过我的脚了。

法海是来找他的，他还是
想让许仙跟白素贞分开。
许仙一听，非常生气。他
说："我知道她是白蛇变的，
可是我妻子心好，对我好，
对别人也好。现在她又怀
孕了，我不会离开她的！"
法海很生气，因为许仙不
听他的话，他就把许仙拉

到金山寺里，不让他回家。

白素贞回家了，她没看见许仙，很着急。她找了很多地方，一天、两天、三天，她每天都出去找丈夫。到了第四天，她终于打听到许仙在金山寺。她很快就带着小青来到金山寺，她求法海，让许仙回家。法海说，让许仙回家，可以。但是白素贞要离开西湖，离开许仙，不能跟他生活在一起。白素贞当然不同意。这时候，法海冷笑着说："你这条白蛇，还是快点离开人间吧，要不，我就不客气了！"

法海不放人，白素贞没有办法，只好和法海打了。他们两个人都有法力。

28

① 求 (qiú) v. beg
e.g., 求求你，这件事别让妈妈知道！

① 金钗 (jīnchāi) *n.*
gold hairpin
e.g., 她头上的
金钗很漂亮。

② 摇 (yáo) *v.* shake
e.g., 他摇摇头，说:
"我不知道。"

③ 流 (liú) *v.* flow
e.g., 杯子倒了，水
流到了地上。

④ 周围 (zhōuwéi) *n.*
surrounding area;
vicinity
e.g., 学校周围有很
多商店。

⑤ 脱 (tuō) *v.* take off
e.g., 我脱了外衣，
因为太热了。

⑥ 堤 (dī) *n.* dyke
e.g., 河堤很高，大
水过不来。

白素贞拿下头上的金钗①，摇②了摇，地上出现了一大片水，很快向金山寺流③过去。金山寺周围④的水越来越多，草不见了，树不见了，房子不见了。很快，大水已经到大门了。法海一点儿也不着急，他脱⑤下身上的衣服，衣服一下子变成一道长堤⑥，这样，水就被拦①在寺门外了。

他们打了很长时间，小青一直在帮白素贞。可是因为白素贞怀孕了，她的法力不如以前大，力气也比以前小，所以她们输②了。白素贞觉得肚子③很疼，最后，她生④下一个儿子，法海用法力把她压⑤在了雷峰塔⑥下面。小青哭了，可是

① 拦 (lán) v. block; hold back
e.g., 他在路上拦住我，不让我回家。

② 输 (shū) v. lose
e.g., 他很不高兴，因为这次比赛输了。

③ 肚子 (dùzi) n. belly, abdomen
e.g., 他肚子疼，因为吃的东西太多了。

④ 生 (shēng) v. give birth to
e.g., 她生了一个漂亮的女孩。

⑤ 压 (yā) v. put sth. under
e.g., 他的照片，我压在那本书下面了。

⑥ 雷峰塔 (Léifēng Tǎ) n. Thunder Peak Pagoda

① 抱 (bào) v. hold/carry in the arms; embrace
e.g., 我一下子把那个小男孩儿抱了起来。

② 寂寞 (jìmò) adj. lonely, desolate
e.g., 房间里只有我一个人，我觉得很寂寞。

她没有办法，只好抱①着白素贞的儿子离开了。

许仙呢？法海让他回家了。可是白娘子不在家里，许仙每天都觉得很寂寞②，也非常难过。他想白娘子，想小青。以前，他们多幸福，多快乐啊！

现在，法海可高兴了。因为，白娘子的药店关门

金山寺

了。没有了<u>白娘子</u>，没有了<u>白娘子</u>的药店，来<u>金山寺</u>的人就多了。家人病了，希望病快点好，人们就会来上香，也会给香火钱。<u>金山寺</u>的香火钱，越来越多；<u>法海</u>脸上的笑，也越来越多。他吃得越来越好，很少练功，所以越来越胖① 了。

后来呢，<u>小青</u>回来了。她在山上练了几年功，法力比以前大了。她来找<u>法海</u>，跟他又打了一次。这次，<u>小青</u>赢② 了。<u>法海</u>输了，他跳进<u>西湖</u>，钻③ 进一只螃蟹④ 的肚子里。<u>小青</u>去了<u>雷峰塔</u>，救出了<u>白素贞</u>，又和<u>白素贞</u>一起找到了<u>许仙</u>。他们一家人幸福地生活在了一起。

① 胖 (pàng) *adj.* stout, overweight e.g., 你吃得太多，所以胖了。

② 赢 (yíng) *v.* win e.g., 我很高兴，因为这次比赛赢了。

③ 钻 (zuān) *v.* get into; make one's way into e.g., 孩子钻到桌子下面去了。

④ 螃蟹 (pángxiè) *n.* crab

Legend of the White Snake

In Southern China lies the City of Hangzhou, a city known for its natural beauty. Each year, many people come to visit the city. West Lake is regarded as the most beautiful place in Hangzhou and is where the well-known and ancient love story of Xu Xian and Madam White took place. Xu Xian was a young man and Madam White, whose real name was Bai Suzhen, was a beautiful young woman. However, this young woman used to be a white snake. Is it possible for snakes to take on a human form? In Chinese legends, they can!

First Encounter

It was a beautiful day in April. Many people came to the West Lake to appreciate the fine scenery. April was the best time to visit the West Lake since the flowers were blossoming, trees had turned green and sunshine showered upon the people. Everyone there was having a good time. Some were spending time strolling along the lake while some were boating. Some were appreciating the flowers and the trees while others were looking at the fish in the lake.

Among the strollers, there were two lovely young ladies. Like the others, they were having a good time taking in the scenery, talking to each other and smiling every once in a while. One of them was in white and the other in green. They were very attractive so many would do a double take as they passed by.

How could anyone know they were actually a white snake and a green snake in human form? The lady in white was Bai Suzhen, the elder sister; the lady in green was Xiao Qing, the younger sister. How could snakes transform into people? Actually, they were no ordinary snakes. They were over one thousand years old and had been practicing magical arts for one thousand years in a mountain. Eventually, they acquired great magic power and were able to transform into beautiful women. Hearing of the beauty of the West Lake, they went on an outing on such a fine day.

It began to rain as they were happily talking to each other. They didn't expect it to rain in the afternoon since the morning was so lovely, so they did not bring an umbrella with them. The heavy rain soaked their dresses and forced them to run for shelter. Suddenly, they noticed that the rain stopped dropping upon them. They wondered what had happened. They raised their heads to see an umbrella above them as a handsome young man was quietly holding it for them. He left himself in the rain holding the umbrella for the two ladies. Bai Suzhen gazed at him and he gazed back. Neither of them uttered a word. Both of them found each other somehow familiar and thought they had met each other before.

Seeing the two of them like this, Xiao Qing couldn't help laughing and asked, "Do you know each other?" They each blushed. Xiao Qing hurriedly explained, "I was joking. I know my sister doesn't know you. May I have your name? Are you from Hangzhou?" The man quickly replied, "My name is Xu Xian. I lived by the West Lake. May I ask what your …?" Xiao Qing interrupted, "I'm Xiao Qing, and this is my elder sister Bai Suzhen. We live in a suburb of Hangzhou. We went on an outing and didn't expect it would rain. Thanks for your umbrella!"

Their conversation went on for a while. The rain stopped. Xiao Qing took her sister's arm and they left. However, Xu Xian still stood there, watching them fading into the distance.

Getting Married

After they got back, Xiao Qing said to Bai Suzhen, "Sister, you gazed at Xu Xian for quite a while today. Do you have a crush on him?" Bai Suzhen didn't answer but she blushed again. After a while, she said, "Well, what's the point even if I like him? We are snakes and he is a human being. We are so different. How could it be possible for a snake and a human to become a couple?" Xiao Qing answered, "I can tell that you like him and he feels the same. Why can't you two live together? We used to be snakes, but now we have turned into humans!" Bai Suzhen thought Xiao Qing's words made sense.

Bai Suzhen and Xiao Qing went to take a stroll along the West Lake the next day, in hopes of meeting Xu Xian again. It didn't take long until they saw Xu Xian approaching them. Xu Xian also wanted to meet the lady in white again. The three of them smiled upon for their second encounter.

They walked and talked for a very long time, just like old friends. Bai Suzhen and Xiao Qing learned more about Xu Xian. His parents passed away and his siblings were all married. So he lived alone. He was an intellectual who read and wrote every day. As his place was near the West Lake, he would take a walk along the lake for a change when he was tired of learning. From that moment on, they saw each other by the West Lake almost every day where Bai Suzhen and Xu Xian would converse for a long time. They enjoyed their conversations and being together. Day by day, they were drawn closer to each other.

Three months later, they decided to get married. On their wedding day, Xu Xian invited many friends. His friends commented that Xu Xian ran into such good luck for his bride was gentle and pretty. After their marriage, Xiao Qing also moved into Xu Xian's house. During the day, Xu Xian would stay at home reading and writing. Bai Suzhen and Xiao Qing would do the housework while chatting with each other. When Xu Xian was tired of reading, the three of them would go for a walk along the West Lake. Together, they lived very happily.

Opening a Pharmacy

One day, Bai Suzhen was doing chores at home when suddenly she heard the neighbor's child crying. It seemed that the child was suffering since the crying was so intense. Bai Suzhen came over to take a look. She found the child had a fever and a sore throat. He was coughing very badly. The child's mother told Bai Suzhen that her son was ill, but she didn't have enough money to see a doctor. The doctor was also far from her place. Bai Suzhen looked at the boy's face and felt his hands. She then went to a pharmacy and brought back some medicine for the boy. The next day, he became well. The boy's mother told many people that Bai Suzhen was a good doctor and she had cured her son. Soon, many people learned the news and came to consult Bai Suzhen for their illnesses. She warmly treated everyone and wrote prescriptions for them.

After a while, Bai Suzhen told Xu Xian that she wanted to open a pharmacy. As Xu Xian was not wealthy, the pharmacy could be a source of income. Moreover, they could help those who couldn't afford their medical bills. Bai Suzhen practiced magical arts for over one thousand years and had gained great powers and medical skills. Some had seen many doctors and took lots of medicine but didn't get well. After they consulted Bai Suzhen and took the medicine she prescribed, however, they recovered in a matter of one or two days. More and more patients came to her, causing their pharmacy to grow day by day. Bai Suzhen never asked for fees from those who couldn't afford it. Everyone liked her. As she often dressed in white, people started to call her Madam White.

The pharmacy business went well. Xu Xian and Bai Suzhen lived a happy life. However, one person became quite unhappy about the situation. Who was it? It was a monk named Fahai at the Gold Mountain Temple. In the past, when people fell ill, their family would go to the Gold Mountain Temple to burn incense to pray for the recovery of their loved ones. They would also donate a reasonable sum of money. Recently, there were fewer people who came to burn incense and worship, and consequently there were fewer donations. Fahai wondered why this had happened. He asked some acquaintances and learned that when people fell ill, they would go to see Madam White, who was so competent that she could cure every illness. Besides, the medicine she sold was inexpensive and she didn't charge fees if people were short on money. With the help of such a kind doctor, people didn't need to go to the Gold Mountain Temple to burn incense and offer donations. Fahai was seething with anger towards Madam White.

The White Snake Showing Her Real Form

The next day, Fahai decided to take a look at Madam White's pharmacy to find out what kind of woman she was and why she was such a skillful physician. When he reached Bai Suzhen's pharmacy, she was seeing a patient and many people were waiting in line outside. Fahai also had magical power. He watched for a while and noticed something unusual: Madam White was not an ordinary person; she had transformed from a white snake!

He stood there for a while and came up with an idea. Then he went to Xu Xian's home and told him, "You wife is not a human. She has transformed from a white snake. You'd better break up with her soon or she would eat you some day." Xu Xian didn't believe him and said, "My wife is the best woman in the world! She is a nice person with a kind heart. Why would you call her a white snake?" Fahai said, "I know you wouldn't believe me. Fine, bring her some realgar liquor. When she takes the liquor, she will turn into a white snake. How about giving it a try?"

Xu Xian didn't want to believe Fahai's words, but he felt uneasy. After Fahai left, Xu Xian thought for two days, during which he had no appetite for food and no desire to sleep. When his wife talked to him, he didn't want to answer. Two days later, he decided to give it a try. He thought that his wife couldn't be a white snake; it would be fine if she drank some realgar liquor. By doing so, he could regain his peace of mind. The following day, he bought back some realgar liquor and lots of food. He cooked dinner and waited for his wife to come back.

Bai Suzhen returned home. Xu Xian said to her gladly, "You have been too tired lately. Today, I prepared your favorite dishes. Let's also have some liquor!" In the last two days, Bai Suzhen noticed that Xu Xian had something in his mind but didn't know what it was. She was worried about him. Seeing Xu Xian was happy, she gladly agreed to join him for some liquor. She couldn't possibly know what was in his mind. However, seeing it was realgar liquor, she put down the cup and said she didn't want to have this kind.

Xu Xian said that this kind tasted good and asked her to try some. Xu Xian tried to persuade her more than once. Bai Suzhen couldn't refuse him and took a sip and thought it wouldn't cause any problem. She didn't expect that after a while, she would have a terrible headache. She knew that there was something seriously wrong. She wanted to send Xu Xian away but she couldn't speak a word.

Xu Xian was standing by the table. He saw his wife's face turning red as if she were ill, so he asked her to rest on bed. Her body then began transforming bit by bit until she became a giant white snake. Xu Xian was extremely scared. He gave out a scream and collapsed to the floor.

Madam White Saving Her Husband

During the night, Bai Suzhen transformed back to her human form. She saw her husband lying on the ground. She came over to take a look, only to find out that he was already dead. Bai Suzhen understood that she scared her husband to death and burst into tears. Xiao Qing came back soon after. She told her sister that she knew the ganoderma mushroom could bring Xu Xian back to life. Ganoderma mushrooms grew on the Kunlun Mountains which were very tall and home to many dreadful beasts. They were far from the West Lake, too. But Bai Suzhen said she was determined to find the mushrooms. She wasn't afraid of either high mountains or the beasts, and certainly not of the long travel. She was determined to bring Xu Xian back to life!

Bai Suzhen started the journey the following day. She went all the way to the Kunlun Mountains in a few days without food or sleep. She defeated the beasts and climbed to the top of the mountains and found the ganoderma mushrooms. Her dress was worn out; her hands and feet bled; she started to lose a considerable amount of weight. She was so exhausted and was in dire need of rest. But thinking of Xu Xian, she didn't stop for rest and soon traveled back home.

Xu Xian was revived the moment he ate the ganoderma. Xiao Qing couldn't help weeping. She told Xu Xian that Bai Suzhen saved his life. In order to revive him, she traveled far away and endured lots of hardships to find the ganoderma. Bai Suzhen's eyes also filled up with tears. She said, "I'm so sorry I didn't tell you that I was a white snake. You were scared to death by me." Xu Xian wept, too. "Now I realize how much you love me. I don't mind that you are a white snake. I want to be with you and never to be away from you."

Later, their life went back to normal. During the day, Bai Suzhen and Xiao Qing went to the pharmacy. Sometimes Xu Xian would help out at the pharmacy; sometimes he would stay at home and study. As before, they still often went to the West Lake to walk around and talk. Several months later, Bai Suzhen became pregnant. Becoming a father-to-be, Xu Xian rejoiced and loved his wife even more.

Flooding the Gold Mountain Temple

One day, Bai Suzhen went to the pharmacy and Xu Xian went to see a friend. On his way, Xu Xian saw Fahai. Fahai came for him and asked Xu Xian to leave Bai Suzhen. Xu Xian was furious and said, "I know her true form was a white snake, but my wife has a kind heart. She is such a good wife to me and nice to others as well. What's more, she is pregnant now. I will never leave her!" Fahai was furious. Since Xu Xian wouldn't listen to him, he captured Xu Xian and forced him to go to the Gold Mountain Temple.

When Bai Suzhen went home, she couldn't find Xu Xian. She became anxious and went to look for him all over. One day passed, then two days and three days. She went to look for her husband every day. On the fourth day, she was finally told that Xu Xian was at the Gold Mountain Temple. She immediately went to the temple with Xiao Qing and begged Fahai to release her husband and let him go home. Fahai said that he could free Xu Xian on the condition that Bai Suzhen would leave the West Lake and never live with Xu Xian again. Bai Suzhen couldn't agree to this condition. Fahai then sneered, "A white snake like you should leave the human world quickly. Otherwise, I will show you what I am capable of!"

Fahai refused to free Xu Xian. Bai Suzhen had no other way but to fight Fahai. Both of them had magical powers. Bai Suzhen took off her gold hairpin and shook it. A large pool of water appeared from the ground and fast flew toward the Gold Mountain Temple. More and more water began to cover the surroundings of the temple. The lawn, the trees and the houses were overcome by water. Soon the flood reached the gate of the temple. Fahai didn't show a single trace of anxiety. He took off his robe and it immediately became a long dyke. The flood was contained outside of the Gold Mountain Temple.

Fahai and Bai Suzhen kept fighting for quite a while and Xiao Qing had been helping Bai Suzhen all the way. However, Bai Suzhen's power and strength were weakened since she was pregnant, so they were defeated in the end. After the fight, Bai Suzhen went into labor and gave birth to a son. Fahai used his magic power to imprison her under the Thunder Peak Pagoda. Xiao Qing wailed but she couldn't save her sister. So she carried the baby in her arms and left the temple.

As for Xu Xian, Fahai freed him. However, Madam White was away. Xu Xian was desolate every day and was very upset. He was missing Madam White and Xiao Qing. They lived such a happy life before!

Fahai was content. Madam White's pharmacy closed so many people came to the Gold Mountain Temple to burn incense and offer donations when their beloved ones became ill. As the temple received more and more donations, there was more and more smile on Fahai's face. He was fed more and seldom practiced magical arts. As a result, he became fatter and fatter.

As time passed, Xiao Qing went back to the temple. She had practiced the magical arts for several years in a mountain, so her powers grew even stronger. She fought Fahai for the second time. This time, Xiao Qing was the victor. Fahai was defeated and fled into the West Lake where he hid himself in the belly of a crab. Xiao Qing went to the Thunder Peak Pagoda and freed Bai Suzhen. The two of them also found Xu Xian. The family lived happily ever after.

一、选择题。 **Choose the correct answer.**

1. 这个故事发生在哪儿？（　　　）

　　A. 苏州　　　B. 上海　　　C. 杭州　　　D. 北京

2. 西湖几月最美？（　　　）

　　A. 三月　　　B. 四月　　　C. 五月　　　D. 六月

3. 白素贞穿什么颜色的衣服？（　　　）

　　A. 白色　　　B. 红色　　　C. 绿色　　　D. 蓝色

4. 小青穿什么颜色的衣服？（　　　）

　　A. 白色　　　B. 红色　　　C. 绿色　　　D. 蓝色

5. 谁带伞了？（　　　）

　　A. 白素贞　　B. 小青　　　C. 许仙　　　D. 都没带

6. 见到白素贞之前，许仙家有几口人？（　　　）

　　A. 四口　　　B. 三口　　　C. 两口　　　D. 一口

7. 白素贞和许仙常常在哪儿见面？（　　　）

　　A. 西湖边　　B. 许仙家　　C. 白素贞家　D. 朋友家

8. 邻居家的孩子哭，不是因为什么？（　　　）

　　A. 发烧　　　B. 嗓子疼　　C. 肚子疼　　D. 咳嗽

44

9. 以前，家里有人病了，人们做什么？（　　　）

A. 去药店买药　　　　　B. 请大夫看病

C. 请法海看病　　　　　D. 去金山寺上香

10. 许仙让白素贞喝了什么？（　　　）

A. 白酒　　　B. 红酒　　　C. 雄黄酒　　　D. 葡萄酒

11. 喝酒以后，白素贞怎么样了？（　　　）

A. 肚子疼　　　B. 头疼　　　C. 咳嗽　　　D. 没有问题

12. 白素贞用什么救活了许仙？（　　　）

A. 灵芝草　　　B. 雄黄酒　　　C. 白酒　　　D. 药店的药

13. 谁知道白素贞是一条白蛇？（　　　）

A. 小青　　　B. 许仙　　　C. 法海　　　D. 他们都知道

14. 法海和白素贞打，他用什么变成长堤？（　　　）

A. 衣服　　　B. 金钗　　　C. 头发　　　D. 帽子

15. 最后，法海去哪儿了？（　　　）

A. 金山寺　　　B. 西湖　　　C. 雷峰塔　　　D. 别的地方

二、判断题：请根据故事内容判断下列说法是否正确，如果正确请标"T"，不正确请标"F"。
Decide whether the following statements are true (T) or false (F).

1. 白素贞和小青已经有一千多岁了。　　　　　（　　）

2. 许仙和白素贞以前见过面。　　　　　　　　（　　）

3. 结婚那天，许仙请了很多朋友。　　　　　　（　　）

4. 白素贞给人看病不要钱。　　　　　　　　　（　　）

5. 大家都喜欢白素贞。　　　　　　　　　　　（　　）

6. 法海常常给人看病。　　　　　　　　　　　（　　）

7. 许仙听了法海的话，让白素贞喝酒。　　　　（　　）

8. 许仙死了，因为他喝了很多酒。　　　　　　（　　）

9. 许仙是小青救活的。　　　　　　　　　　　（　　）

10. 白素贞和法海打，她输了，因为她怀孕了。　（　　）

三、选择填空。 **Choose the appropriate words to fill in the parentheses.**

1. 她们正高兴地说笑，（　　　　）下起雨来了。早上天气好好的，她们（　　　　）中午会下雨，所以没带伞。雨下得很大，不一会儿，她们的衣服就（　　　　）了，她们只好到处跑，想找个地方（　　　　）。她们跑着跑着，突然觉得头上的雨（　　　　）了，这是怎么回事呢？两人（　　　　）一看，头上多了一把伞。

A. 没想到　　B. 躲雨　　C. 突然　　D. 抬头

E. 停　　F. 湿

2. 她知道，出了大问题。她想让许仙出去，（　　）已经说不出话了。许仙站在桌子旁边，看到妻子的（　　）越来越红，像生病了一样。他想让她到床上（　　）。可是，他看到妻子的身体在变，一点点地变，一会儿就（　　）了一条大白蛇。许仙吓（　　）了，大叫了一声，倒在了（　　）。

A. 脸　　B. 变成　　C. 地上　　D. 可是

E. 坏　　F. 休息

3. 第二天，白素贞出发了。她一路上不吃饭，不睡觉，几天后（　　）到了昆仑山。她打跑了野兽，（　　）山上最高的地方，找到了灵芝草。她的衣服（　　）了，手脚流血了，人也（　　）了很多。她非常累，真想休息一下。可是她心里（　　）许仙，一会儿也没有休息，很快就回家了。许仙吃了灵芝草以后，一下子就（　　）了。

A. 瘦　　B. 活　　C. 爬到　　D. 想着

E. 终于　　F. 破

四、连线题。 Match.

1. 请根据故事内容连线，组成完整的内容。

A. 到处   a. 办法

B. 听到   b. 病了

C. 倒在   c. 哭声

D. 没有   d. 跑

E. 好像   e. 地上

2. 根据故事内容为下列事物选择合适的搭配。

A. 脸   a. 湿了

B. 衣服   b. 开了

C. 树   c. 绿了

D. 花   d. 停了

E. 雨   e. 红了

五、请根据故事内容给下列句子排列顺序。
Put the following statements in order according to the story.

A. 可是有一个人不高兴了。他是谁呢？他就是金山寺的一个和尚，叫法海。

B. 有这样的好大夫，当然就不用去金山寺上香了。

C. 白娘子很厉害，什么病都能治好，卖的药也不贵。要是看病时没有钱，她就不要钱了。

D. 法海不知道这是为什么。他出去问了几个认识的人，这才知道原因。

E. 可是最近几个月，来金山寺上香的人比以前少多了，香火钱也越来越少了。

F. 药店的生意很好，许仙和白素贞的生活也很幸福。

G. 别人告诉他，现在人们病了，都去找白娘子。

H. 原来，寺里的香火钱越来越少，就是因为这个白娘子啊！法海很生气。

I. 因为以前，人们家里有人病了，就会到金山寺来上香，还会给很多香火钱。

1. 请根据图片说说这幅图应该放在这本书的第（　　　）页。

2. 图片中都有什么人物?

3. 图中的人物在做什么?

4. 他们的心情怎么样?

5. 请你用中文或英文给这幅图加一个简单的标题说明。

练习题答案 **Key to exercises**

一、选择题
1. C   2. B   3. A   4. C   5. C
6. D   7. A   8. C   9. D   10. C
11. B   12. A   13. D   14. A   15. B

二、判断题：请根据故事内容判断下列说法是否正确，
如果正确请标"T"，不正确请标"F"
1. T   2. F   3. T   4. F   5. T
6. F   7. T   8. F   9. F   10. T

三、选择填空
1. C   A   F   B   E   D
2. D   A   F   B   E   C
3. E   C   F   A   D   B

四、连线题
1. A -d, B-c, C-e, D-a, E-b   2. A-e, B-a, C-c, D-b, E-d

五、请根据故事内容给下列句子排列顺序
F-A-I-E-D-G-C-B-H

唉	*interj.*	āi	(used to express sadness or regret) alas
安静	*adj.*	ānjìng	quiet, calm
办法	*n.*	bànfǎ	solution
抱	*v.*	bào	hold/carry in the arms; embrace
不安	*adj.*	bù'ān	uneasy, disturbed
传说	*n.*	chuánshuō	legend
床	*n.*	chuáng	bed
担心	*v.*	dānxīn	be worried
到处	*n.*	dàochù	every place; all places
堤	*n.*	dī	dyke
肚子	*n.*	dùzi	belly, abdomen
对方	*n.*	duìfāng	other side; other party
躲	*v.*	duǒ	hide, duck
发烧	*v.*	fāshāo	have a fever
法力	*n.*	fǎlì	magic power
风景	*n.*	fēngjǐng	scenery
感情	*n.*	gǎnqíng	emotion, feeling, sentiment
古代	*n.*	gǔdài	ancient times
和尚	*n.*	héshang	Buddhist monk
湖	*n.*	hú	lake
互相	*adv.*	hùxiāng	mutually; each other
划船	*v.*	huáchuán	boat

怀孕	*v.*	huáiyùn	be pregnant
急	*v.*	jí	be anxious
寂寞	*adj.*	jìmò	lonely, desolate
家务	*n.*	jiāwù	chore, housework
脚	*n.*	jiǎo	foot
金钗	*n.*	jīnchāi	gold hairpin
金山寺	*n.*	Jīnshān Sì	Gold Mountain Temple
救	*v.*	jiù	save, rescue
咳嗽	*v.*	késou	cough
昆仑山	*n.*	Kūnlún Shān	Kunlun Mountains
拦	*v.*	lán	block; hold back
雷峰塔	*n.*	Léifēng Tǎ	Thunder Peak Pagoda
厉害	*adj.*	lìhai	serious, intense
练功	*v.*	liàngōng	practice magical arts; practice one's skill
聊	*v.*	liáo	chat
灵芝草	*n.*	língzhī-cǎo	ganoderma mushroom
流	*v.*	liú	flow
流血	*v.*	liú xiě	bleed
绿	*adj.*	lù	green
漫	*v.*	màn	overflow, flood; run over
没关系		méi guān-xi	it doesn't matter …
美丽	*n.*	měilì	beautiful, pretty

52

面熟	*adj.*	miànshú	(of a person's appearance) familiar
庙	*n.*	miào	temple
摸	*v.*	mō	feel, stroke, touch
南方	*n.*	nánfāng	south
暖	*adj.*	nuǎn	warm
爬	*v.*	pá	climb
螃蟹	*n.*	pángxiè	crab
胖	*adj.*	pàng	stout, overweight
破	*v.*	pò	break, damage
其实	*adv.*	qíshí	actually; in fact
求	*v.*	qiú	beg
伞	*n.*	sǎn	umbrella
散步	*v.*	sànbù	take a walk
嗓子	*n.*	sǎngzi	throat
上香	*v.*	shàngxiāng	burn incense and worship
蛇	*n.*	shé	snake
生	*v.*	shēng	give birth to
生意	*n.*	shēngyi	business
湿	*adj.*	shī	wet
实在	*adv.*	shízài	indeed
试	*v.*	shì	try
瘦	*adj.*	shòu	thin
输	*v.*	shū	lose
帅	*adj.*	shuài	handsome
抬头	*v.*	tái tóu	raise one's head
疼	*v.*	téng	hurt, ache
脱	*v.*	tuō	take off
温柔	*adj.*	wēnróu	gentle and soft; sweet

吓	*v.*	xià	frighten; be scared
现形	*v.*	xiànxíng	reveal one's true features
香火钱	*n.*	xiānghuǒqián	donations to a temple
想法	*n.*	xiǎngfǎ	idea
小伙子	*n.*	xiǎohuǒzi	young man
雄黄酒	*n.*	xiónghuángjiǔ	realgar liquor, liquor mixed with foul-smelling realgar to drive away snakes
压	*v.*	yā	put sth. under
摇	*v.*	yáo	shake
药店	*n.*	yàodiàn	pharmacy
野兽	*n.*	yěshòu	wild animal; beast
夜里	*n.*	yèlǐ	night
医术	*n.*	yīshù	medical skill
赢	*v.*	yíng	win
运气	*n.*	yùnqi	luck, fortune
挣钱		zhèng qián	make money; gain profit
治	*v.*	zhì	cure, heal
周围	*n.*	zhōuwéi	surrounding area; vicinity
主意	*n.*	zhǔyi	idea
桌子	*n.*	zhuōzi	table, desk
钻	*v.*	zuān	get into; make one's way into

项目策划：韩　颖　刘小琳
责任编辑：韩　颖
英文编辑：吴爱俊
设计指导：isles studio
设计制作：isles studio

图书在版编目（CIP）数据

白蛇的传说 ：汉、英 ／ 许晓华改编 ． -- 北京 ：华
语教学出版社，2016
（"彩虹桥"汉语分级读物．2级 ：500 词）
ISBN 978-7-5138-1000-5

Ⅰ．①白… Ⅱ．①许… Ⅲ．①汉语－对外汉语教学－
语言读物 Ⅳ．① H195.5

中国版本图书馆 CIP 数据核字（2015）第 183038 号

白蛇的传说

许晓华　改编

张　乐　翻译

＊

©华语教学出版社有限责任公司
华语教学出版社有限责任公司出版
（中国北京百万庄大街24号　邮政编码 100037）
电话：(86)10-68320585　68997826
传真：(86)10-68997826　68326333
网址：www.sinolingua.com.cn
电子信箱：hyjx@sinolingua.com.cn
北京虎彩文化传播有限公司印刷
2016年（32开）第1版
2022年第1版第5次印刷
（汉英）
ISBN 978-7-5138-1000-5
002200